# SHUT
# UP
# SLOW
# DOWN
# LET
# GO
# BREATHE

# SHUT UP SLOW DOWN LET GO BREATHE

MARCUS MCCANN

Invisible Publishing
Halifax & Picton

Library and Archives Canada Cataloguing in Publication

McCann, Marcus, 1983-, author
Shut up slow down let go breathe / Marcus McCann.

Poems.
Issued in print and electronic formats.
ISBN 978-1-926743-93-6 (softcover).--ISBN 978-1-926743-96-7 (EPUB)

I. Title.

PS8625.C365S58 2017 C811'.6 C2017-901969-4
C2017-901970-8

Edited by David O'Meara

Cover and interior design by Megan Fildes | Typeset in Laurentian
With thanks to type designer Rod McDonald

Printed and bound in Canada

Invisible Publishing | Halifax & Picton
www.invisiblepublishing.com

We acknowledge the support of the Canada Council for the Arts which last year invested $20.1 million in writing and publishing throughout Canada.

Canada Council for the Arts Conseil des Arts du Canada

ALSO BY MARCUS MCCANN

POETRY BOOKS

The Hard Return
Soft Where

CHAPBOOKS

Shut Up Slow Down Let Go Breathe
Labradoodle
Raw Rind: Sad Songs for Occasions
The Glass Jaw
Town in a Long Day of Leaving
Force Quit
The Tech/Tonic Suite
petty illness leaflet
Basement Tapes
Heteroskeptical
So Long, Derrida

PRAISE FOR MCCANN'S EARLIER WORK

From the startling metaphoric seize of the opening, the lines propel themselves full throttle, through sonic reverberations and imaginative mimesis.

– Stephanie Bolster, John Newlove Award Citation

Each publication by McCann is perfectly rendered so there's not an ill-considered rhythm or word or syllable.

– Pearl Pirie

PRAISE FOR *THE HARD RETURN*

Marcus McCann's *The Hard Return* is a musical, sensual delight, a plurality of voices both human and instrumental.

– Vanessa Herman, *The Malahat Review*

Not a syllable is wasted; rather than teach an austerity of pleasure, it encourages luxuriating and loitering in the back alleys of his poems. One day, someone will get the idea to use this book as a break-up letter, because woven into it are the molecular sounds of bodies that regret nothing that was physical, transcendent, important.

– Daniel Allen Cox, *Plenitude*

The density of McCann's lines are incredibly packed, sassy, sensual and wry and move at lightspeed, nearly light-headedly so, delighting in an openness and sense of play. In *The Hard Return*, McCann writes poems that pilfer and magpie, reshaping them into his own fantastic entities.

– rob mclennan, *Jacket2*

Poetry is too often predictable. This book is not.

– Billeh Nickerson, *Xtra*

PRAISE FOR *SOFT WHERE*

This stunning book explores the possibilities of bringing image to life, written in the language of the people and soaked in a heart of sapphire. The jury was intoxicated by this book.

– Gerald Lampert jury citation

This is poetry for a new age.

– Ronnie Brown, *Canadian Bookseller*

A collection of throbbing, muscular poems.

– Paul Gessell, *Ottawa Magazine*

Sexually, technically, and technologically charged, Marcus McCann's poetry is invigorating and accessible to anyone with an imagination.

–Ashley Dick, *The Leveller*

## TALK OF SAFETY IS REALLY TALK OF DANGER

*; come, poor Jackself. I do advise*
*You, jaded, let be; call off thoughts awhile*
*Elsewhere; leave comfort root-room; let joy size*
*At God knows when to God knows what;*

— Gerard Manley Hopkins

## Lyric for a Little Lullaby

We are currently experiencing a delay
westbound at Bay.
Efforts to resume
regular service
are underway.

Do not rush when you hear
the subway door chimes.
You may experience
longer than normal travel times.

We are currently experiencing a delay
westbound at Bay.
Efforts to resume
regularly scheduled service
are underway.

We apologise for the delay.
A response crew is on its way.

BABY IN A MOMENT I GOT BOOMS FOR YOU TO HEAR

## Funk from the Man-Man Cave

Pre-dawn penumbra of heavy air. Ogre aura
folded like extra wools.
Wherever its magma, tephric drift

dusts its weepy, limping sulphurs, its smell
part alluvial mud, part dorm fridge. Breezes, love
of nomadics and the tin labyrinth of HVAC

carry the worst downwind. But not at night: a potpourri
reaches its long forearm into our doffed civvies, sheets
and the porous pulps our faces face.

Pre-sleep cuddling breaks
but doesn't vanish, hovering mid-air
in mixing particulate, seamed

with the impetuous ease of those beloved—
and which too soon will recite new lines
*return air, supply air, exhaust air*

and carry on.

## In Praise of the Sun-Cloud-Rain-Lightning Icon

Pictograph of our actual days
with a chance of everything.

Patience, honey. Air will send
live updates.

Sit still with your unsatisfied heart.
I know you want

"an answer"
but

oh, to abandon odds
for a thumbnail hinting
all options are equal

so none is exactly likely.
Or in the long view,

given infinite skies
the probability of all events
tends toward one.

But no. To abandon odds
is to abandon panic, panic
that cancels picnics,

sticky bike trips to nowhere.
The wheel has one bright spot
and that is enough.

Add your applause

to the tentative plaudits
of its makers:

imagine the colloquium
at the Conference of New Meteorology

—convened in a field
of thistles, bugged wind,
rim lit up in pre-storm glow—

to adopt for the future
an ideogram of doubt

and sing its song
maybe, maybe.

## Safesound Soft Foam Earplugs, Neon Green

Slug, glowworm, forgetful flowerbuds
which slip distance in. Doorjamb, airbrake, dock

bumper between neighbours. Self-help
remedy, snorers' lovers' little lovers

asleep in a deeper alcove. Twos

of resisters—check this early reversal—
in daylight shove the world right up to your eyes

like its sediment sagged off in a kid's hand. Like a closet
after laundry, overfull,

overbright. The odd kid picked focus
as his very most wished for mutant trick

knowing the world is a pitcher
with five leaks and no stopper.

Fellow perceivers,
you can't tamp the gurgling down,

but you can cut a smaller
pinhole. You prolly already know

inside silence
is disordered, prickly

optimism. As in, some eyes water, some
wonder. I don't but

if I thought the soul
weighed a number of grams,

I'd put foam plugs on the scale's
other plate, best method for hearing

yourself breathe, trumpet muffler,
puffed budgie,

almost
ear mask—

## On Not Being Able to Sing

Voice like an underwater turbine choking
on American English. A voice *manmade*. Rock Hudson

scarred his vocal folds—on purpose, at twenty,
oh Hollywood!—to craft a tone in oratory

like a crew over the next dune thumping on drydocked
boat hulls. It filled the lake of his singing voice with slag.

Rock Hudson and The Little Mermaid
have this thing in common. As for me,

I don't have one song I can barter with.
Little stomped-on harmonica. Puff of noise

you can squeeze from a rabbit with all the melody of a poem
about Marcus McCann written by Marcus McCann.

Can all coyotes sing, or do some mouth their howls
like I do the national anthem? The song inside me—

not to get heavy—is a theme that circles me
Alzheimerally. If that's a word. I can't always express

the upbeat choruses that tent on the cliff's edge
of my solitary and social selves. I apologize

for smothering the fun out of karaoke. But not really.
I peel packing tape from the skin of audiences:

imagine the foreboding when, after singing
*The Greatest Love of All* in rhythmless monotone,

the host calls my name to sing—wait for it—
*The Greatest Love of All* again in the second set.

## Shores of One Island

Through bramble, we caught poplars exhaling. White fur
soap bubbles, hundreds, as if pure light detached from flora

could with only an inkling of an earthly arc canoe
    through air.
They weren't in my *idea* of the beach

but let's give ourselves to their whimsy.
That was the first lesson. We undressed and lay. Tiny yogis

in ermine coats headed for transcendence: they carried
    themselves
the way we'd hoped to treat our day's vacation.

I want to touch the world so lightly.
To hammer it home, we made a game of metaphor:

crumbs of clouds, porcupines sculpted
from milkweed, souls en route to an orgy...

and I thought we'd hit the groove of lyric. But
    it sedimented
in the literal sense—breeze rhinestoning us

with unstoppable, obsessive fluff everywhere we sweated
plus our mouths and eyes. And when we stood, we saw

seeds had filled the shallows of the lake. We shuddered
at the sight:
endless, gooseshit coloured, and sort of waving at us.

But these are different shores of one island.
There is no way off. And as we packed, the poplar seeds,

slowburning like a guitarist at a campfire
whose one drunk song is *Helpless*, went on and on and on.

## Wreck of a Street Racer, Etobicoke

Hardly a car. More a corrugated, ingrown bale of machine,
a metal lasagne.
What the end credits of *Carrie* roll over. Tough as Rizzo
from *Grease*.
The lawn of Kipling Collegiate growing a skin tag. A goitre
on a trailer hitch.

The driver's side—door, yes, but the car's whole left face
peeled off, its boot
3-D anatomy sketched by a realistic hand pressed
for space.
An X-ray of a suitcase, a pinched nerve, a gut's worth of
plumbing.

Whatever roaring, steaming road mess this wreck is a
souvenir of, now it's ornament.
I stand and watch it like a cell phone kiosk students
stream around.
None rise above baseline distaste. The staff who planned
this—earnest administrators?
Public funders of a police pilot? A charity for the
advancement of scared straight?—

don't need me to tell an audience primed for metaphor
    what it means.
But what does *what it means* mean? I'd like to set this
    wreck on the lawn
of the Board of Education, draped in a banner reading
    *pedagogy*.

## Never Straighten Is My Advice

*Psychoprojective New Year's Letter to Galiano Island*

Twilight spreads like nut butters. Ideally
fairy lights. Ideally a breeze carrying neighbours.
Ideally kibbutzing kids at dinner, verdant and pearled
ruffage, rye loaves that flake like stressed pets
and white, red, rose, Burgundy, verde. Like you

sparkling and still. Ideally your feet aren't anvils
but updraft, your brain and heart aren't storms
but transformer and transformer joined by sizzling
wire. Shift work, bawdy work, a firework
is emotional labour. Exegesis. Listening is work

but Kitty I'm tuned to your rumbles.
The future came forward to spook you, light
and smoky as a woman in a green dress saying
*Baby in a moment I got booms for you to hear.*
Never straighten is my advice. Ideally

a toast that sprawls from voice to voice like a ribbon
you coil and uncoil only because it is soft
and its softness comforts you. Did you ask
for fortune in an accessible format
because it's here. Ideally

disordered ideation. Imagine our adult
daughters colluding. Ideally rest, messes, rest.

# REVENGE BY LIVING

//

A tool to stitch strips
in an overplucked

couplet. Rest

but not really. Your knees
scooching air

from a sleeping bag.
Did you know

a little breath
can make serum?

Glyph which says
pause

knowing pause
can hide an

independently
beautiful, parallel
little leer

can hide momentum,
which wants you to
and does not want you
to stop. // watches

poor human us,
lazy, concrete lovers

and quietly pries open
poemish soundbites. I wrote

"an // independently / beautiful,
parallel / little leer"

thinking of a dam
you and a wind
can walk on.

I'm not saying mystery,
I'm just sort of

incompetent.
"Sort of // incompetent."

Think nap
when a nap won't take,
anticipation, pre-photo

preening, the handsome

fidgety glottals
before a pickup starts,

half
rest, quarter rest, stroke

stroke, in fill,
stand-in.

## Use the Smallest Chainsaw Suitable for the Job

Greg chokes its motor, hangs
its suffocating butt end
off my hand.

Backhoe ear bone. A metal
ferret snoozing. A rumour
about your love

which is true. I get a noseful:
greased, sheeted tin,
shed shoes

and a note of charred pepper.
At thirteen, I was surly
about this work

because my soft parts embarrassed me.
Now I let a motocross
attitude

be my guide to Revenge by Living.
I raise a flag over the sunlit,
friction

blacked, hashmarked chain
and into the leaves
it launches

an anthem wicked and normal.
Gloves like silt under
pressure.

Another name for backhoe
is *rear actor*.
Dad says

the first rule of getting out
of a hole is stop
digging.

When I bury the saw's hooked teeth
in saplings three dimensions
shift.

The idea of "weekend" sits
on the blade's edge
like a man

climbing into your lap who wants
you to fuck him.
Woodchips

roughen the underbrush,
Greg's sweats.
The first rule

of getting out of a hole is
to ask am I in a hole?
Boots

with a note scrawled in mud
scrawl in mud and
sawdust.

The note is nonsense or I don't
understand it but probably
it's nonsense.

## Derailleur, Derailleur

Haltering clatter of a bad grind
you've been living with
resolves—just resolves—
unprompted, unearned
as if the ease
you're going to the island to bathe in
arrived early, the world
pouring in from a spigot
in the sun and this one's
on the house.
Even the road bows
to give you the slightest
and most leisurely decline. And maybe
it's the glass corridor kennelling wind
but maybe it's you, throwing open
double doors of solid air. And maybe
it's a sweatslick on your neck,
but maybe the whole
goddamn week
is waving from the back of your skull
like tiny strips of tinsel. I like
to be good in public, so you know
I have dark habits. Part of the mind
commits arson,
controlled burn, even now,
the road newly paved, your bike
icing a sweet rich chocolaty cake.

## Easy Living While Everything Else Moves

Gemma's lit on Banff Ave. as night falls,
as a certain curtain falls over our sharper

powers of perception. She's rocking
a shirt that unseen revelry spit up on her lawn

screenprinted, "I'm retired, do it yourself." The inner voice
of the heavily high added rabbit ears.

She's twenty-two. Gemma catalogs her distaste for men
who float though. *Come back in ten years*

*when you're nice*. Nearly everyone grown to maturity
passes through being twenty. Ding. Young men

grapple with feelings about my sex ad.
*Lie down with snowboarders, wake up*

*with fleece*. Ding. I try to ungum the spritz bottle of my
    empathy
with the warm cloth of a J, and I see a red balloon

moseying the sidewalk at the gentle to downright dopey
end of the decisiveness spectrum. But for the nipple

where the air got in, it would spin
in perfect circles. Your heart will invent new worries

if the normal ones resolve.
Attaboy. At last

night flops down like a hiker on a couch
and we all help pull her boots off.

## Cover Letter

A graceful arrangement of the baubles of enthusiasm.
Why you matter, retail. An explanation of how
you were gingerbreaded from the dough of their firm
    at birth.

Your motto is *avoidio missteppus*. Your interest in grammar
grows abnormally. You long for font synergy.
Your other motto is *Chuck Norris does not apply for jobs; jobs*

*apply for Chuck Norris*. In take two, you trim
your illustrious history to six slick bullet points. Later,
you cut the least glimmering facet and lean on autocorrect

like it's a crisis counsellor. The person you are describing
is awesome, you realize, or pathological. Your draft
    reflects you
the way a can of Diet Coke does. You delete *If I were a*
    *question*

*I would be burning* because it is an awkward topic sentence.
In draft three, you shift the Most Polished Paragraph
to the Power Position. It is above you. You count to ten.

You mamabird rebuttals into the beaks of their imagined
objections. You pour in Professional Register
as if from a tap of weak beer. Sincerely, you write, sincerely.
    Sincerely…

## In All Your Days May Three Books Be Your Works

*Psychoprojective New Year's Letter to San Luis Obispo, California*

No party, but not alone. Connected by a thought's
thinnest wisp, literal paper, to the Brainiac Brigade.
And connected too by spittle to the cracked
spine of a daddy-type. Stars on white shoulders,
hot tub jets lower. There's a light problem

in my "version of events" but this rock tablecloth
has a lot to offer. For now fields taking a beating
love the one crop. Where it meets sky, rim
for days. Cali's into edging. You think of your book,
it's tidal. A new year can soak the night's

napkin like a sudden spill, or seep in. Fireworks
are a type of works. Earthworks. Levees. New growth
forest is a type of works. It's as dark in Celsius
as Fahrenheit. A good plan is to listen
to the neighbour's hoot hoot rodeo:

one sound in sex is the sound of fish on a dock
flopping. One sound is gasping. The T-chart
breaks down where one sound is a breakwater
of invectives, hectoring, and semi-tender diminutives,
and the other is your lullaby as it dies.

There's thinking and then there's wonder, and the sluttier
the x, the deeper the y is the night's puzzle.

## Not to Get Cutesy, but This Is Definitely a Message from My Id

When you squeeze the rubber ball of public
blood pressure, something about your heart
gets diagnosed. Take the staple gun.
What does its one-syllable telegram say?
Crack shot. Slingshot. Shiny as a hip flask,
heavy as the knot in your throat before
oratory. The part of your id you can photocopy
has a message for you, something urgent
and repeatable. Fake stable. Clutch purse
of the earnest, the obsessed, the cash strapped.
Don't mistake the high, unironic register
of paper, its shaggy aegis like shaved
meat, for the gun, with its earthy rhythm
of compression, heartbeat starter, CPR.

## Village of the Darned

Days pass like hot air
from an ill-sealed house.

Sky is agitating
for reform. Yesterday's

slight, outlined:
snobby cotton mass
like mould floating on juice

and waiting to be swept up
in the weather.

Not that air wants
anything: it has behaviours.

Amounting to bolts:
pale, layered, aphasic

and accreting
extra humps.

A chart of markets
in the long view. Off

couplings, even.
Soft calendar
to lie on.
Shedding log. I wrote

a Yelp review
of skies:

*It's cool to see*
*where all our power*
*comes from.*

*On what prescription*
*am I? Oh yeah, its vastness!*

Dear laundry, each mistake
is a sour smell
I can barely distinguish.

You see lovers
slide in and away
as if off a continental shelf.

No one should be made
to watch a man choose poor
entertainments.

But you are laziness
piled on laziness,
you say meh

with a shit-
rigging shrug.

You will
stay still and still

summer
will come to you!

# CRUISING IS PUBLIC SERVICE

## Filament, Branching Out

Sex not as aerobics but as two streams
meeting in a little V—low volts—say, a man is kneading
my back as if he's grating hard cheese, and his knuckles

grip a patchy thatch—my body is me
so I agree with its choices, but years ago it picked
for a hobby a cross between raising Chia Pets

and weaving, and at first, this little tuft asked questions
by raising only one finger, timid,
now it's bold as a glade between farms—say his pause

resolves in a tug, his face saying
*Underwater my feet caught a whisper of kelp*
*and it's unnerving*—and I want to say

you are feeling the spindly wings I grew
in second puberty, my unshame, hirsute abandonment
of the expected script, undepilatated me,

prenatal hair returned like wisdom
revealed only by a second example—I do not say
aging is applying a dry rub, no. As for him

he pulls as if pulling a raft's rip cord—me as safety rep,
don, attendant with my warm—warmer—insulated
inner parts—I yelped, not a word, but a syllable,
    how could I not?

## The Jeweller's Made Uncountable Examples

*Once it is reduced to a photograph, is all nudity in a way a surprise? Is it possible to catch the medium itself blushing?*
— Regina Skelton

Settled in a corona of late night
bedroom more muddy
Madawaska effluvia
than bachelor pad,

sit for a portrait of the self
as sea cucumber.

To accrete its themes,
search skin tag online.

No, don't. Search nuzzling sponge.

I get it.
Sex is magical,

in that it requires
misdirection.

So cue the bi

sected shot: on one hand, tender
exposure

—sweet as a drunk palm
finding yours on a night walk—

on the other, impervious catcall
unsolicited bravado
in darkling air.

Look,
you say, *I don't want
to be recognized*,

but don't you?

Oh, dear stranger *qua* stranger,
I hear the frequency
on which you hum.

I've seen the world's one
dick pic.

Until I cottoned on

I thought the pleasure
was merely

putting your fingers
through a whole cake.

Now,

inching
my phone up my chest

as if peeking at a pocket pair—
through the flush
I hear

*Put down your guard,*
*your smarmy talk, whatever*
*good you try to do*

*I'm pointing at you,*
*and you, all of you,*

*all of you, every one.*

## Poem for Scott Who Gave Me Conjunctivitis

Scrapper, through swollen open lids
before the vanity—cramped, lit
like discount grocery—I tilt my skull back,
squint, scope out this bacterial
shiner *sacré coeur*
eye patch. A nightbird
laid a heavy pink shit in my socket.
A camera is a bad eye, my eye
now a bad camera. You cannot see
and also unsee. The microbes
cruising the Jacuzzi of my intraocular
fluids flooded my rims
under cover of night. I was not attuned
to fences, tracing a scrotal
seam to lay my tongue
like a wet dog inside
your sphincter. Espresso
and muskox flank, dried blueberry
gym bag, allspice, tobacco
flower, flange, newel, rained-on
gravel, olive brine. Heavy
sled on ice moan in octave zero. Privacy
is not a thing in this world,
we're too close. Last night scuppers
naively from me, I am a blown-
out photo, flooded motor, my eye
an ecstatic report of a boatman spotting
light.

## There Are No Tense Problems at the Great Imaginary

*Psychoprojective New Year's Letter to London*

The Last Word and an Uneasy Understanding
please. No ice in the Understanding.
At your elbow, a stranger flicks his plastic
and your bill disappears. Some trick.
Dark like a bedroom lit by sidelight throws

pouty shadows on the waitstaff, hired
for their killer knowing glow. Fire *works*,
is employable. Don't get ideas. If there's a litmus
it's that she could fill a Life's Like That
till the end of her days. May all our worst vignettes

be anonymized. Morning regrets
will bunch around your body like bedding.
You and your boyf will bed him who's been perving
on you, that's certain. *Imma love your love bites*
*if you let me undress you*, his stare said. His stare said

*There'll be ricochets and mutual plunder*
*and your hard arms are gonna leave marks.*
You got latitude that comes with status, let's keep
perspective. Outside, Saigon Pharmacy accepts
your drug plan, Happy Massage accepts walk-ins.

If anything is a radio it's your mandible. Only Lang Syne
is calling you Auld and anyway you murdered it.

## Poem for the Morning

Recall
his slept-on curls
face half hid
under groggy
longing half
lit with slants
of kid-like sun
frame stoic
as an electric
transformer
midfield
a slow responder
your protective
liquids
intuitively
bubble for
as he stumbles
over an aphorism
looking down—
I'm only sketching—
a paraphrase—
there's grace
in not being
seen. When I wake
I think, this
better be good.
Among pitches

blank for shortage
of self-esteem
offstage dishonesty
cranky pranking
or sheer need
for control
are those who—
if this has the air
of convenience it isn't—
are overwhelmed.
Is it hotter
to plan pleasure
or be taken
in its musky
arms and thrummed?
He on his elbows
leans, elastic,
floppy, sincere,
reeking. Some days
I feel like rice
thrown at no one.
A pebble
in a mouthful
of pop rocks.
He says no
parachute
sail, windsock.

## On Receiving Robert Earl Stewart's "The History of Baseball" from a Lover by Email

Mornings you imagine your job as dragging
contaminated dirt out of a mine
one shovelful at a time. The day is a white bird
you can clean the slick off of
but so what? Dear lover,
every time you send me a poem

my chest cramps.
I have renamed
my two lungs Poetic Diction
and Interpersonal Feeling. The swelling
makes me feel worse about smoking.

I don't know what it means to die.
Or: I know, but I don't *really* know. I twigged
to the difference reading a poem you sent me
whose theme is you can still be surprised
by your lover after ten years. I know that

but I don't *really* know it.
What motion sensor did this poem set off
in the fog of your morning? How did you feel?
How did Robert Earl Stewart feel?

I'd like to know how I feel—
and I'm chopping at that bit obliquely
this morning, the day leaning over me
like a child who finds you lazing in bed
and asks you to punish
her brother. I'm writing this poem for you
so quickly it is like a hostage
photographed with today's newspaper.

And maybe that's all I mean—
the glare on a portrait under glass.
The speaker—a heterosexual, a father!—
is also reading that David Berman book!
On the nightstand over there, that very book!
You understand, right?
The best glow is searchlight *and* fog.

## Poem with Three Naps and No Plot

We get the naps we deserve, not the naps
we need. After nights before deadline
hours I'd not turned my mind to

show up. A bilge pump
for light would be handy
but either way sleep hugs me

like the synthetic fur
inside a barbecue cover.
Choices grow exterior. Other times

The One Drunk Night I keep running into
cabs me to a part of town
called Frat Life. If I'm lucky

I'll bolt home before it gets weird.
All tomorrow's APBs: my body curls
the juice my brain floats in

thickens. Remind me, at what stage
of plot does a novelist
express the highest and most noble

feeling? A slow
bureaucracy unwinds me
the next hour so revealing

so ominous it must be
redacted as it's written. If I lie still
I might be found. In the third act,

the day lets itself in
to watch my passive, slack
zonked-out love and me

and if we weren't asleep
in our slither of fluids
I might hold this afternoon

up and inspect its bezels and seams
and pencil in conclusions
with a happy buzz

like an appraiser with an oddity.

## Sex at Thirty-One

Here's hunger's sweet spot, extra dough,
and a summary of my competencies,

is what I thought the year would be.
Under its canopy, I vowed to string

enough fairy lights end to end to make waver
the dominant view. That and get off.

It was overly lofty. Bulbs burst not from weakness
but because I dragged them over patio tiles.

As for my body, I was a bad tenant
in an okay apartment. Onto the year's dartboard

landed a missive from a neighbour to please
revolve the venetions before, well, I guess he'd caught

full frontal of me undoing layers of manners
from a man like the laces of a thigh-high boot.

By July, days were also peaking
in their thirties; I scored among the uniformly

over forty at the beach's ramble, that itch a fifty-fifty
ticket, mostly a gift. I flagged my heart out,

learned cruising is public service. Cruising *is* public service.
As winds chilled, my bed pegs split. I lived between frames

and during the interregnum,
my meetup with college life pulled back curtains

on cravings for order I didn't realize had cured in me.

Unsettled is how I felt. Like how one bad haircut collapses
the capillaries of our self esteem. The clinic

endorsed my theory of love as infection cluster.
On that topic: to a man who predated this birthday
I said let's be bandmates on life's

slutty bus tour. By December I'd red pencilled my plan
for outsmarting my own asshole habits. Paper

wore until it ripped. Winter was a smothering ruffle
of short days and long johns. Loafing around

my actual days, my style shrunk from cool
to "cool dad," I guess that's not a sex thing.

I got really into Stevie Nicks. The year

wrapped around itself like a marriage in a headlock
and before I blacked out I caught a glimpse

of the world as I thought it was, a public
of confidantes, conspirators, lieutenants

undressing from their idiot clothes,
us sleazebags, saddos and weirdos, knots of lovers, chains

and chains of clippered buds, impossible to preserve,
seriatim, stamen, John Stamos, satyr, sweat, salt.

## To a Lover, Shy of His Attachments

If I got inside your head—a dumb idea—
I would walk through like a man at a market

with no money. I prefer it out here,
where you flash your high beams

on me, for example, and your smirk is like a smooth
rock I treasure regardless of its weight.

You're not cruel, I admit it's hard
to know how to arrange all my feelings.

You've run out of vases. Do you know,
a heavy black glitter pours out of everything

you touch? I see it on other men.
I'm okay with that. Listen, there's a whole roster

of ways to love you. A whole club. We field
together. Some weeks I just watch and cheer.

TALK OF SAFETY IS REALLY TALK OF DANGER

## Resignation Letter

Pour your feelings into the cement mixer of restraint.
Delete the vignettes of your crying jags, anger
at management—discount the post-work, day-drunk
unloading on your friends by the probability
they like your kvetching. Yes, you watched your boss's quirks

dry into burrs. She ground ambition out of you
like orange pigment out of a beetle. Let go. Be resigned.
You were a blade's whir until stopped by a rock. Yes, facts
hamstrung you. "Processes" needed "overhaul."
The job's promise dimmed like a sitcom

leaning on gimmick. At some point, it flipped the trip switch
of your ego. Repeat after me: *I am a house*
*and quitting is a circuit breaker.* You are extracting yourself
from your job like a good tooth from a bad mouth.
From your former job, I mean. What a lovely phrase.

## Petroleum Safety Conference
*Banff Centre, Banff, Alberta*

Uncuttable boots, pinnies IDing one
as Material Not To Be Crushed. First
aid packs I'd be antsy for amateurs
to apply. Risk is sinking like heavy gas
to the Innovation Display Room,
where product has liquified to AutoCAD
drawings on slick LCD. Talk of safety
is really talk of danger. Like camping

with today's kids, it's BYO infrastructure.
So that booths collapse is likely unwelcome
metaphor-wise. Nevermind. For fun, catch
harness demos. Between, the plaza is so calm

it's like everyone able has bolted for help,
and MIA riffs with samples: shotgun, cash register.

## To Whomever Checks the Office's General Email Account

Phalanx of the literally ascending
but proverbially stuck. Vladivostok elevator

to the less successful floors of Business in America.
Among us one who tracks info at, office at, questions at

like a teen collects and doles out bowling shoes. Support
at. Dear madam, dear operator, if it concerns you,

a mix of thanks and unease follows me
like a hunter who doesn't know his rifle's empty.

Please administer to us who are angry, bratty, bored,
whiny, irregular, mentally ill, unusually inventive,

truly abusive or angling for a refund.
That is, all of us, virtually. On what wavelength

do you wait for petitions? Oh reactor,
ghosts appear to believers,

not to us who could
use a break. In your sign-off

pop the collar of the nameless: the team,
customer service, x or y branch, on behalf of, or

thank you plus two carriage returns
like a thin signet of white smoke.

## Labradoodle: An Essay on David McGimpsey

*i. Monster movies are a metaphor for parenting. Or I guess I mean they're a metaphor for having parents*

Her parents gave us a rug hook portrait
of young Burt Reynolds. I took it as a reminder
of the moment in horror movies
when our heroes realize that the monster—

or alien, or serial killer, or deadly virus—
is adapting. Her parents were adapting.
No more picture frames with laser-cut
texts of friendship poems, no more

bath bombs. All bets were off. Luckily,
just like in horror films, her parents' worst,
most fatal flaws remained. When they dropped
by unannounced, again, with their Yorkie

Labradoodle cross-cross breed, she told them
she never loved them. Later, the survivors hugged
as the music swelled, but a twist in the final scene
left room for a sequel. Or, excuse me, "a franchise."

*ii. Three years ago, I was not quite ready to use the word Labradoodle in a poem*

It's like that time I found, in the memo folder
of my BlackBerry, the one-word memo
*Cocktapus*. I thought about it for a long time,
how it got there, what I was trying to say

to my future self. *Dear self. Cocktapus.*
Much later, I added two more words:
*Cocktipmus Prime*. You can be physically
ready for sex but not emotionally ready,

I learned in Grade Eight. It was confirmed
the day I crossed out April on the office
calendar and wrote *Cocktober*. I just hadn't
figured out what part of misery

"Labradoodle" stood in for. Now I think I know.
Every day is a David McGimpsey poem,
and it's half Golden Lab, and half whatever
"doodle" stands for. It is/is not good news.

### *iii. Okay, we've lived here for a month, it's time to start cleaning the bathroom*

The art of negotiations seminar I took in business
college did not prepare me to negotiate
which one of us should clean which bathroom.
That the guest bathroom had fewer toothpaste marks

but must, must smell like lavender at all times
was just one of the *Sophie's Choice*-type tradeoffs
I realized too late. I realized too late that I should have
put the title of this poem in quotation marks.

Never take credit when it is obvious you wouldn't
have arrived there on your own. I could teach a business
course called Things It Is Better Never to Learn
than to Learn Too Late. A registration requirement

would be total ignorance of the course material.
I would barely teach. I would be the best prof.
On the first day, I would review the syllabus,
then let the students out after fifteen minutes.

*iv. A primer on David McGimpsey for those who have never heard of David McGimpsey*

The poet laureate of the tragic, the mentally
unwell, and poor dressers, all who opted out
of the grading curve of the mall parking lot.
Patron ~~saint~~ of the dive bars of Montreal.

Every poem unfolds like an episode
of *Full House*. Funny, and then, wham!
a surprise life lesson. And a hug.
Except, rather than the cast of *Full House*,

it's you doing the hugging, and the man
you're hugging is a prickly SOB
who doesn't want to be hugged, he will tell you,
even though deep, deep down he does.

That and the Olsen twins. People say
David McGimpsey is the guy who writes
funny poems. Which is a little like saying
hey, he's the guy with the really funny cancer.

## Be Respectful. Basement Laundry Is Shared

Never renoed. Walls the color of a lint bin
soaking in chocolate milk. Industrial linoleum
so committed to being there, it doesn't peel
but wears thin in strips. Machines
like a white neck under a grimace, visibly stressed. No one

can live in splendid isolation. The laundry
is *shared*, meaning *those who own own it.*
At group, for full effect you need a few:
drunks on a tom-tom working themselves
into a lather, a neighbour playing cop toggling

between coaxing and beration, offstage
greasy creaking of a medic shifting her weight.
I aim for odd hours; there is enough noise
in the lobby of the living without talking to strangers.
Imagine multipliers on the smell—

already anti-bacterial, syrupy
and normothermic. I wouldn't hang around
but for signs warning both *we are surveilled*
and if our clothes are lost, nicked
or otherwise wrecked *no one is responsible*.

## Last Night Pulls Back the Veil

A fissure in your thoughts
opens. Last night

you left unsettled
as in, the bill. You watch

through the dashcam of your panic
an earlier you

lurching from the Sutton Arms. Shit
shit shit shit

shit. Breath takes a vacation
from your vacation.

You are making a disorienting
entry into a lake.

If you'd meant to ditch
your debts youdda picked a grander scale.

Your wicked pickling finally
turned to bile. Your cheeks tipple.

The slow recital of your virtues drops
its elbows on a shelf

of piano keys. Let me try an I statement:
my past is full

of bad behaviour. That's not confession
just context, chagrin

without consequence. I get filled with stupid
embarrassment

like a toy truck filled with air everywhere
it's not plastic.

## His Nail Polish Pulls Back the Veil

Strut. Flounce.
Saucy Boss.
Invincible Glint.
Giggles.
Fried Green Tomorrows.
Uvula.

Heartichoke.

Fruit Pit. The Ramble. Gay Lea.
Brand New Sneaks.
Just Got Paid. Mission Creep.
                                        Simony.
French Boundaries.
All That Bickers Is Gold.

Bruised Ego.

Aftercare.

Largesse. Fade to Black.
Catscratch.
                All Nighter. Dirty Knees.
Clouded by Emotions. Stormy. Mojo Juice. Lingering Jingo.
Denouemint.
                  Longtail.

Tammy Fey.
Running Mate. Hacked Jean Jacket.
Overkill.
            Frosty Reception. Kensington Sidewalk Standoff.
The Unbearable Lightness of Green.

Pillow Talk.
Total Bodem.
                  Sleeper Hit.
Chewing the Scenery.

Alarm Belle.
                 Ohm Wrecker.

## Reciprocating Saw, or How I Learned to Steal Bikes at a High Volume

On an Annex porch, I let rip its craw
on a U-lock, like a rifle butt licking my pit—
I tell friends *Think, portable band saw,*
*butch turkey carver*. Can you picture it?—

chassis vibrating, its shake a marimba
on my rib like a boyfriend in seizure, grit
rubber on my skin. Its *naaaaah*
echoes, its tone grows bossy. I interpret

its bitch and wail, its catcall and applause
by math of a lesser science. This is legit
love I have on my hands, hands slackjaw,
arms rope. In its deepening groove, the blade submits

to an alternating current, withdraws
and replants. The lock kicks, chuckles. Splits.

## Little Fury

*The brown-headed cowbird is a brood parasite, meaning it lays its eggs in the nests of other birds. Cowbirds have been known to kill the host chicks, in order to keep competition for resources low.*

—The Penguin Birds of Alberta Handbook

Hear the song
of the electric fence
and understand
what wired is.
Song of guessing
on gameshows
if guessing
had aftermath.
Song of tech
when tech fails.
No tune: its high
mistakeable tone
ear infection
over shortwave
is the song of the world
after news.
In a Pogo cartoon
two cowbirds discuss
the national debt.

~~Cowbirds~~
~~scope out~~
~~as many as ten~~
~~before choosing~~
~~a nest~~
~~to lay eggs in.~~
Between migrating
with bison or raising
baby cowbirds
I might pick bison
though the mere
thought of that choice
puts me on edge.
Ever feel
like you're living
on the massive
matted flank
of a mammal?
In *Titus Andronicus*
Tamora lives
on the massive
flank of her grief.
Medea.
Some noise.
Is a cowbird
watching now?

Though I find
bird lore
tough to trust
when she sings
revenge
is the register.
Generations
lock in
around the rough cut
of their violence.
So much is air
to fly through,
little fury.

## Zombie Apocalypse Kit

Rugged machetes, one with spike and bladed
hook, one serrated—gruff, multi-purpose
tools, receipt-thin, balanced as a cochlea,
light as fracking gas, sharp as clam shells,
crafted for their smack and clang, the noise
a graft of cracked bat and wooden spoon
in wet cheese. Conjured by a slacker with an Idaho
"a." Conjured by anyone on Amazon.com.
Not included: water filters, cans, blankets
or fodder for first-level barricades. Nevermind.
Imagine heaving a lung of acrid, flatulent
air. Imagine grappling, cold skin sloughing off,
imagine cleaving skulls. So what if you can't return
to the compound, even through quarantine.

## A Sound You Hear in Your Molars

This vignette: lifting
my salted face from a mall loading dock

where at five a.m. even the respiration
of supply chain management pauses

for yogic stretches. Material for an opera
house. Past shipping, the visitor's lot

is empty, its painted notches a blueprint
for a suburb, a diagram of a network

for delivering cold, clean water. It doesn't.
As flashbacks to snot crying

through A Bad Scene ping
I pick up an intermittent, alternating

song, song of sick, persnickety kitsch dragged
over gravel, like a hacksaw's shudder

drawn across a playground slide, its chorus long odds
gelling into horror. Looped like embroidery thread

in a mawkish braid. Looped like bad family
habits. I'm tempted to think it's something else

than what it is: an anti-bird bird machine
replaying a record of an animal provoked

to distress. In hours
when the aperture of my ego is projecting

as close to one-to-one as the settings
of that little instrument allow, I'd admit

I can't shake the phases of sneering
and self-regard. Shut up. Slow down. Let go.

Breathe. An urge blooms to swap
into my day life a ringer, a boy pulping Coke cans,

hero of a pulp panning coked boys, a man
sturdy as a cabinet cartwheeling downhill.

## Heart Filled with Little Matters

You can carry a grocery bag
by its strap like a violin case
or a bucket. Set it down
as you would a baby seat
or like you've got to get these rocks
off your lot. You can take care or be rough
or both. Re-potting a fern,
dropping its crumbling
brown brain on newsprint.
Coaxing and yanking. New soil
like a black velveteen
hood. You can look
with or without wanting, a dark line
like a high-water mark
settling under your ring. You will give it
what it needs even if not gingerly.
Don't mistake attention for affection.
You can live in the world
without love for it. It's not a disaster
just a mess, heart filled with little matters
and resolution unclear to all, or to me at least.

## Acknowledgements

Earlier versions of many of these poems appeared elsewhere, and I am grateful to the editors and others involved with the magazines and websites which printed them. "To Whomever Checks the Office's General Email Account", "Funk from the Man-Man Cave" and "Easy Living While Everything Else Moves" first appeared in *Riddlefence*; "Wreck of a Street Racer" first appeared in *Truck*; "On Not Being Able to Sing" and "Poem with Three Naps and No Plot" first appeared in *The Steel Chisel*; "Cover Letter" first appeared in *The Puritan*; "In Praise of the Sun-Cloud-Rain-Lightning Icon" and "//" first appeared in *Jacket2*; "Poem for Scott Who Gave Me Conjunctivitis" first appeared in *Plenitude*; "The Jeweller's Made Uncountable Examples" first appeared in *This Magazine* and subsequently in *Best Canadian Poetry 2015*; "On Receiving Robert Earl Stewart's "The History of Baseball" from a Lover by Email" first appeared on the Chaudiere Books National Poetry Month website; "Resignation Letter" first appeared (briefly) on the *Arc Poetry Magazine* website; "Shores of One Island" first appeared in *Matrix Magazine*; and some of these poems have also appeared in the chapbooks *Labradoodle* (Chaudiere Books) and *Shut Up Slow Down Let Go Breathe* (Dusie).

## Notes

"Lyric for a Little Lullaby" is a found poem, borrowing common language used by Toronto Transit Commission staff over the subway intercom, intended to be sung.

"Shores of One Island" is for Lucy Cappiello and Jonathan Valelly.

"Wreck of a Street Racer" was written for the students of the Grade 12 Writers Craft Class at Kipling Collegiate in the spring of 2012.

"Never Straighten Is My Advice," "In All Your Days May Three Days Be Your Works," and "There Are No Tense Problems at the Great Imaginary": Several earlier psycho-projective New Year's letters appear in *Soft Where* (Chaudiere Books, 2009). The game is to imagine what friends might be doing on New Year's Eve. These three "letters" were written for K. Louise Vincent, Steven Ruszczycky, and Brandon Perlberg, respectively.

"//": A pair of forward slashes are commonly used to mark a stanza break when quoting a poem.

"Cover Letter": "Chuck Norris does not apply for jobs..." borrows from a popular internet meme. This poem was written for classmates who participated in OCIs (an odd form of employment speed dating available to law students) in 2012.

“Village of the Darned” borrows lines from two Yelp reviews of the Hoover Dam.

“On Receiving Robert Earl Stewart’s “The History of Baseball” from a Lover By Email” refers to “The History of Baseball” a poem in Stewart’s *Something Burned Along the Southern Border* (Mansfield Press, 2009) and David Berman’s book *Actual Air* (1999, Open City Books).

“Poem with Three Naps and No Plot”: APB is an acronym meaning “all-points bulletin.”

“Sex at Thirty One”: There is a lot I left out.

“To A Lover Shy of His Attachments” is a reworking of Shakespeare’s Sonnet 20.

“Resignation Letter” is for Mark Schaan.

“Petroleum Safety Conference”: The conference is a real thing. It took place at the Banff Centre (formerly the Banff Centre for the Arts) in May 2014.

“Labradoodle”: These poems are “chubby sonnets,” a favoured form of David McGimpsey.

“His Nail Polish Pulls Back the Veil” is a list of fictional nail polishes.

“Little Fury”: Cowbirds are brood parasites, meaning they scoop eggs out of other birds’ nests and replace them with their own; Tamora in Shakespeare’s *Titus Andronicus* seeks revenge for the death of her son.

“Zombie Apocalype Kit”: Is indeed available from online retailer Amazon.com.

The epigraphs in “Little Fury” and “The Jeweller’s Made Uncountable Examples” are fictional.

## Thanks

We get to choose what family means to us. Many thanks to Leigh Nash and the Invisible Publishing family for believing in this weirdo little book, to David O'Meara for editing it with generosity and openness, and to all the writers who have pushed me lo these six long years, especially rob mclennan, Pearl Pirie, Paul Vermeersch, Hoa Nguyen, and Andrew Faulkner. Shoutout to the Law Poets Society. Shoutout to the Banff Centre.

I have been sustained during the writing of this book by friends, lovers, and the loose associative and interconnected network of sexual communities in Toronto and elsewhere. Love to Mikiki, Anthea Black, Carly Boyce, Michael Erickson, Hayley MacPhee, Mallorie Malone, Krista Nerland, Erin Secord, Jessica Whitbread. And to Paul Sutton, subject of so much of this book, *I look at you and I would rather look at you than all the portraits in the world...*

INVISIBLE PUBLISHING is a not-for-profit publishing company that produces contemporary works of fiction, creative non-fiction, and poetry. We're small in scale, but we take our work, and our mission, seriously: we publish material that's engaging, literary, current, and uniquely Canadian.

We are committed to publishing diverse voices and experiences. In acknowledging historical and systemic barriers, and the limits of our existing catalogue, we strongly encourage Indigenous and writers of colour to submit their work.

Invisible Publishing is also home to the Bibliophonic series, and the Snare and Throwback imprints.

If you'd like to know more please get in touch:
info@invisiblepublishing.com

Invisible Publishing
Halifax & Picton